LMH OFFICIAL ~~DICTIONARY~~ OF
Ja ~~maican Reg~~ ae

DANCEHALL STARS

VOLUME 1

Compiled by

K. Sean Harris
&
L. Mike Henry

LMH PUBLISHING LIMITED

Compiled by: K. Sean Harris & L. Mike Henry
Cover Design: Sanya Dockery
Typeset & Book layout: Sanya Dockery
Photographs provided by: Buzzz Magazine, Peter Simon, Roy Sweetland, Stacey Bethel, reggaeportrait.com, Dennis Brown Trust and Imani Music Jamaica

Published by: LMH Publishing Ltd.
Suite 10-11, Sagicor Industrial Park
7 Norman Road, Kingston C.S.O; Jamaica
Tel: 876-938-0005
Fax: 876-928-8036
Email: lmhbookpublishing@cwjamaica.com
Website: www.lmhpublishing.com

Printed in China   ISBN: 978-976-8202-58-1

NATIONAL LIBRARY OF JAMAICA CATALOGUING-IN-PUBLICATION DATA

Harris, K. Sean
   LMH official dictionary of Jamaican reggae and dancehall stars / compiled by K. Sean Harris & L. Mike Henry

      p. : ill. ; cm. – (LMH official dictionary series)

ISBN 978-976-8202-58-1

1. Reggae musicians – Jamaica – Dictionary   2. Dancehall (Music) – Jamaica- Dictionary
3. Jamaica - Biography
I. Henry, L. Mike   II. Title   III. Series

781.646 - dc 22

CONTENTS

INTRODUCTION

Jamaica is a remarkable island. It is mind boggling the way this tiny dot on the map has had such a huge impact on the world through music. Reggae music is a global phenomenon that has penetrated markets as diverse as Japan – the biggest market for reggae outside of Jamaica – Norway, France and the United Kingdom to name a few. It has given birth to an offspring – dancehall – and has been successfully fused with other genres such as R&B, Hip Hop, Rock and Soca. Reggaeton, a form of Latin American dance music, also blends reggae and dancehall. The late great Bob Marley transcended reggae music to become one of the world's most recognizable cultural icons.

Reggae music has become a billion dollar industry and even in the ever-evolving musical landscape where the emphasis is now on digital downloads via the internet due to the steady decline of CD sales, reggae is still a popular, inspirational and relevant genre. Reggae (and dancehall) have given birth to films such as 1972's brilliant *The Harder They Come* which starred reggae icon Jimmy Cliff, *Rockers* which was released in 1978, 1997's *Dancehall Queen* which featured dancehall ace Beenie Man, 2010's *Rise Up*, which featured reggae greats such as Sly Dumbar and Lee 'Scratch' Perry, and 2012's *Marley*, a documentary on the life, music and legacy of Bob Marley.

The dancehall queen competition, where women vie for the title by dancing to the dancehall songs of their choice, has evolved into an international competition and contestants from all over the world now enter the annual event. Past winners have included dancers from countries outside of Jamaica such as Japan and the United States.

It was amazing to see some of our athletes, particularly Usain Bolt, celebrating their historic, record-setting performances at the 2008 Summer Olympics in Beijing, by doing then popular dance moves such as the 'Nuh Linga' and the 'Gully Creepa', effectively showcasing dancehall culture on the world's biggest athletic stage.

This dictionary, the first of continuous volumes to follow, takes a brief look at some of Jamaica's musical stars, both past and present. We have included the pioneers, the legends and the members of the new generation who have, through their music, made a major impact both locally and internationally.

A

ANTHONY B

Anthony B is the stage name of this Rastafarian reggae singer, born Keith Blair on March 31, 1976, in the parish of Trelawny. Anthony B adopted Rastafarian beliefs as a teenager, a decision which was not well-received by his family. He refused to give up his new religion (and his dread-locks), and relocated to the home of his aunt and uncle in the city of Portmore. He is a member of the Bobo Ashanti branch of the Rastafarian movement. Anthony B released his debut album *Real Revolutionary* to critical acclaim in 1996.

He has since released several albums, including *Seven Seals* in 1999, *Street Knowledge* in 2003, *Higher Meditation* in 2007 and *Rasta Love* in 2011 which featured collaborations with Kymani Marley and Gyptian. Anthony B tours extensively in Europe and North America, and is known for his passionate, high energy performances.

B

THE INVINCIBLE
BEANY MAN
The 10-Year Old D.J. Wond

IS REAL

AH

LEGEND
the best of
BOB
MARLEY
...and the WAILERS

Bunny Wailer

Rootsman Skanking

WORLD BEAT INTERNATIONAL

THE BEST OF   PART.2
BOUNTY KILLER

 SELECTOR RONDON

BU
BANT
RAS
GO
SO

BEENIE MAN

Beenie Man, born Anthony Moses Davis on August 22, 1973 in Kingston, is one of the most popular and respected dancehall entertainers. A prodigious talent, Beenie Man was involved in the music industry from a young age when he won the Tastee Talent contest in 1980. He recorded his first single, "Fancy Face", when he was eight years old and released his debut album, *The Invincible Beenie Man: The Ten Year Old DJ Wonder,* in 1983. He has had a stellar and exciting career since, highlighted by his fourteen year feud with fellow ace DJ Bounty Killer; collaborations with international acts such as Janet Jackson, Mya and Wyclef Jean, and winning the Grammy Award for his album *Art and Life* in 2000. The 'King of the Dancehall' – he was officially crowned on Dancehall Night at the 2009 staging of

Reggae Sumfest. He got married to Michelle Downer, aka D' Angel, in a lavish ceremony in August 2006. She is an entertainer and his rival Bounty Killer's ex-girlfriend. Though the marriage failed, the union produced a son, Marco Dean.

Beenie Man remains relevant and continues to perform at a high level whether in the studio or on stage.

BERES HAMMOND

Beres Hammond, born Hugh Beresford Hammond on August 28, 1955, is a reggae singer known primarily for his romantic lover's rock. A native of the parish of St. Mary, he grew up listening to his father's collection of American soul and jazz, including Sam Cooke and Otis Redding. He was further influenced by the native sounds of ska and rocksteady, in particular the music of Alton Ellis. Hammond participated in local talent contests from 1972-1973, which led to his first recording, Ellis' "Wanderer". Hammond formed his own record label, Harmony Records in 1985, for the release of his album *Make a Song* which had two Jamaican chart-toppers, "Groovy Little Thing" and "What One Dance Can Do". The latter, along with a duet with Maxi Priest, "How Can I Ease the Pain", began to break

Hammond into the international market. He garnered interest from major recording labels such as Elektra Records on the strength of hits such as "Putting Up a Resistance", "Strange" and "Tempted to Touch". Hammond recorded several albums in the 1990s as well as several compilations, establishing himself as one of the top lover's rock artistes. His first album of the new millennium was 2001's *Music is Life* which featured an appearance by Wyclef Jean. Beres Hammond remains one of the most beloved reggae singers and tours extensively, doing shows in both his native Jamaica and abroad.

BOB MARLEY

Robert Nesta 'Bob' Marley OM (February 6, 1945 – May 11, 1981) was a singer, songwriter and musician. He was the lead singer, songwriter and guitarist for the ska, rocksteady and reggae bands: The Wailers (1964 – 1974) and Bob Marley & the Wailers (1974 – 1981). Marley remains the most widely known and revered performer of reggae music, and is credited for helping to spread Jamaican music to the worldwide audience.

Bob Marley was born in the small village of Nine Mile in the parish of St. Ann. His father, Norval Sinclair Marley, was a white Scottish-Jamaican. Norval was a Marine officer and captain, as well as a plantation overseer, when he married Cedella Booker, a Jamaican, then eighteen years old. In 1955, when Marley was 10 years old, his father died of a heart attack at age 60. Marley suffered racial prejudice as a youth because of his mixed racial origins and faced questions about his own racial identity throughout his life. In 1963, Bob Marley, Bunny Wailer, Peter Tosh, Junior Braithwaite, Beverley Kelso, and Cherry Smith formed a ska and rocksteady group, calling themselves "The Teenagers". They later changed their name to "The Wailing Rudeboys", then to "The Wailing Wailers", at which point they were discovered by record producer Coxsone Dodd, and finally to "The Wailers". By 1966, Braithwaite, Kelso, and Smith had left The Wailers, leaving the core trio of Bob Marley, Bunny Wailer, and Peter Tosh. After a conflict with Dodd, Marley and his band teamed up with Lee 'Scratch' Perry and his studio band, The Upsetters. Although the alliance lasted less than a year, they recorded what many consider The Wailers' finest work. Marley and Perry split after a dispute regarding the assignment of recording rights, but they would remain friends and work together again.

The Wailers' first album, *Catch a Fire*, was released worldwide in 1973, and sold well. It was followed a year later by *Burnin'*, which included the songs "Get Up, Stand Up" and "I Shot The Sheriff". Eric Clapton made a hit cover of "I Shot the Sheriff" in 1974, raising Marley's international profile. The Wailers broke up in 1974 with each of the three main members going on to pursue solo careers. The reason for the breakup is shrouded in conjecture; some believe that there were disagreements amongst Bunny, Peter, and Bob concerning performances, while others claim that Bunny and Peter simply preferred solo work. Marley's best known hits include "I Shot the Sheriff", "No Woman, No Cry", "Exodus", "Could You Be Loved", "Stir It Up", "Jamming", "Redemption Song", "One Love" and, together with The Wailers, "Three Little Birds", as well as the posthumous releases "Buffalo Soldier" and "Iron Lion Zion". The compilation album, *Legend*, released in 1984, three years after his death, is the best-selling reggae album ever (10 times platinum in the US), with sales of more than 20 million copies worldwide.

Marley died at Cedars of Lebanon Hospital in Miami, Florida, on the morning of May 11, 1981, at the age of 36. The spread of melanoma to his lungs and brain caused his death. Marley was inducted into the Rock and Roll Hall of Fame in 1994. *Time* magazine chose Bob Marley & The Wailers' *Exodus* as the greatest album of the 20th century.

In 2001, Marley was posthumously awarded the Grammy Lifetime Achievement Award, and in 2006, the State of New York renamed a portion of Church Avenue from Remsen Avenue to East 98th Street in the East Flatbush section of Brooklyn "Bob Marley Boulevard".

In 2012, Marley, a feature-length documentary about his life, was released. With contributions from Rita Marley, The Wailers, and Marley's lovers and children, it also tells much of the story in his own words.

BOUNTY KILLER

Bounty Killer, known also as 'The Warlord' and 'The Five Star General' was born on June 12, 1972 in Kingston. His birth name is Rodney Basil Price. The last son in a family of nine, he grew up in the rough neighbourhood of Seaview Gardens. He originally performed under the name Bounty Hunter, but later changed it to Bounty Killer. He has been a household name in Jamaica since 1993, and in 1996, his hit single "Fed Up" was banned by the Jamaican government. He has done collaborations with international acts such as No Doubt, Mobb Deep and the Fugees. His legendary rivalry with Beenie Man was given a break at the 2010 staging of the popular annual summer event Fully Loaded, where they performed on stage together to close the show, much to the delight of the crowd. It remains to be seen how long this truce will last. Bounty Killer is revered by many of his peers and upcoming artistes. He is known for his hard work in fighting poverty and helping new acts. He is also the founder of the dancehall collective known as The Alliance.

Viewed by many as the most controversial and provocative dancehall star, Bounty Killer, after over 17 years, is still one of the most popular dancehall acts around.

BUJU BANTON

Buju Banton, whose birthname is Mark Anthony Myrie, was born on July 15, 1973 in Kingston. He was one of fifteen children born into a family who are direct descendants of the Maroons. At the tender age of 12 he began performing under the moniker 'Gargamel' and released his first single "The Ruler" in 1987. He changed his stage name to Buju Banton and in 1991, linked up with ace producer Dave Kelly, and together, they made some memorable music. The singles "Bogle" and "Love Mi Browning" were massive hits in Jamaica, the latter spawning controversy due to the lyrics of the song which spoke of Buju's preference for light-skinned women. He responded quickly and admirably, releasing "Black Women" which spoke of his love for dark-skinned beauties. 1992 was a phenomenal year for Buju as he broke the late great Bob Marley's record for the greatest number of number one singles in a year. That same year also saw a great deal of controversy regarding his hit single "Boom Bye Bye" due to its homophobic content – the song proclaimed that homosexuals should be shot and killed. Buju Banton embraced Rastafarianism in 1994 and released his landmark album *Til Shiloh* in 1995 to critical acclaim and commercial success. The album successfully blended conscious lyrics with a hard-hitting dancehall vibe and reflected his new spiritual beliefs. The brilliant *Untold Stories* followed, earning him comparisons to Bob Marley in some quarters. *Inna Heights* was released in 1997, followed by *Unchained Spirit* in 2000 and *Friends for Life* in 2003. He returned to dancehall basics with 2006's *Too Bad* which spawned several hit singles, re-establishing Buju as a prominent hit-maker on the dancehall scene. April 2009 saw the release of *Rasta Got Soul*, Buju's ninth studio album, which featured the hit single "Magic City" and which was nominated for a Grammy award in the Best Reggae Album category.

His stellar career was interrupted by his arrest in Florida for a conspiracy drug charge in December 2009. He pleaded not guilty and went to trial. The jury failed to come to a unanimous verdict, and there was a mistrial. There was a second trial in 2011 and he was convicted on three counts and sentenced to 10 years.

Despite his tribulations, Buju Banton is cemented in the minds of reggae lovers everywhere as one of the most notable artistes of his time.

BUNNY WAILER

Bunny Wailer, born Neville O'Riley Livingston on April 10, 1947, is a world renowned reggae singer, songwriter and percussionist. Though born in Kingston, young Bunny spent his early years in Nine Mile, St. Ann. It was there that he first met Bob Marley. He was an original member of the reggae group The Wailers, along with Bob Marley and Peter Tosh. The Wailers became an international success, with most of the focus on Bob Marley. Bunny eventually left the group to pursue a solo career and became more focused on his spiritual faith. He identified with the Rasta-farian movement, as did his former band-mates. Bunny Wailer has recorded primarily in the roots style, in keeping with his usually political and spiritual lyrics. Wailer's stellar solo career includes hit albums and singles in a number of different styles. 1981's "Rock 'n' Groove" was a departure from his typical roots style and showcased his talents as a dancehall artiste. Bunny Wailer has recorded more than 20 albums, earned eight Grammy nominations and won the Grammy Award for best Reggae Album in 1990 for *Time Will Tell,* done as a tribute to Bob Marley, and again in 1995 for *Hall of Fame*. Wailer is also known for his powerful live performances. His 1982 performance at the benefit for the Jamaican Institute for the Blind was recorded and released as a critically acclaimed live album. Notorious for hating to tour, especially abroad, he broke with tradition entirely in 1986 and embarked on a world tour. His first appearance in the United States took place in Long Beach, California, with his later appearance in New York recorded for the 'In Concert' video. He has since performed at venues throughout the world, and continues to draw capacity crowds to this day.

BURNING SPEAR

Burning Spear , birthname Winston Rodney, was born on March 1, 1948, in St. Ann's Bay. He entered the music business in 1969, after fellow St. Ann native Bob Marley introduced him to producer Clement Dodd of the esteemed Studio One label. That meeting resulted in Spear's first recording, "Door Deep" and his first two classic albums, *Burning Spear* and *Rocking Time.*

Building on this foundation, he went on to record for Island Records in the 70s, releasing three albums, *Marcus Garvey*, *Man in the Hills* and *Garvey's Ghost.* These searing releases saw the emergence of Burning Spear as an international artiste whose artistic vision began to permeate popular culture around the world. These were followed up by *Hail H.I.M* for EMI Records and set the stage for a prolific string of releases through the 80s and 90s such as *Rasta Business, Resistance, Mek We Dweet, The World Should Know, Fittest of the Fittest* and the Grammy Award winning *Calling Rastafari*.

Burning Spear has been nominated for a total of twelve Grammy Awards, and he has won two Grammy Awards for Best Reggae Album: the aforementioned *Calling Rastafari* in 2000 and 2009's *Jah is Real*.

A certified musical legend, Burning Spear's career has already spanned three decades and shows no sign of slowing down. His live shows are legendary, regularly lasting over two hours and delivering more energy than many reggae and rock and roll acts half his age.

He has been based in the United States since the mid-90s and was awarded the Order of Distinction in the rank of Officer by the Jamaican government on October 15, 2007.

Through his music, Burning Spear has been able to unite and uplift people all over the world with his messages of peace, love and black unity.

C

CAPLETON

Capleton, born
Clifton George Bailey III
on April 13, 1967, in
the parish of St. Mary,
is a Rastafarian reggae and dancehall
artiste who is known for his energetic
performances and songs hitting out against
social injustices and homosexuality. As a
member of the Rastafari movement, Capleton,
also known as 'The Prophet' and 'The Fireman',
belongs to a number of different orders
called Mansions of Rastafari. Capleton first
arrived on the scene in the late 80s with a
slew of hits laced with raunchiness and gun
lyrics, such as "Number One Pon De Look
Good Chart", "Woman We Lotion" and
"Bumbo Red". They were all chart toppers,
firmly establishing Capleton as a dancehall
hitmaker. In 1992, he released the single
"Alms House" which solidified his place as
one of dancehall's brightest stars. He followed

that up with "Music is a Mission" and "Tour", which was a big hit in the United States after it was remixed with rap star Method Man of The Wu Tang Clan. Unlike other artistes that tried to detach themselves from their earlier work, Capleton readily acknowledged and incorporated his already established raunchy hits in his thesis of conciousness. His latest album, *I-Ternal Fire*, was released in 2010. He is the brother of Jamaican track star Aleen Bailey.

CHAM

Cham, born Damian Beckett in Kingston on February 24, 1977, is a dancehall artiste famed for his 2006 single "Ghetto Story" from his major label debut album of the same name. He was previously known as Baby Cham until 2005. He is still called 'Baby Cham' by most of his fans from around the world. Blessed with a deep baritone and a commanding hard-core delivery, Cham had his first two major hits in late 1996, "Funny Man" with Mr. Easy and "Joyride" with Wayne Wonder on Dave Kelly's Joyride rhythm. "Another Level" done with his then idol Bounty Killer was a chart topper in 1999 as was "Ghetto Pledge" recorded on Dave Kelly's Bug rhythm. His ambitious debut album, *Wow...The Story,* was released in 2000. Throughout his career, Cham has collaborated with many hip-hop and R&B artistes such as Foxy Brown, Carl Thomas, and T-Pain, and had two huge hits with R&B songstress Alicia Keys and rapper Mims respectively.

He was busy in 2012 and uncharacteristically released four singles in one year. Usually he only releases two or three singles. The four songs are "Wine", "Tun Up", "Back Way", featuring his wife 'O' and "Drop It".

COCOA TEA

Cocoa Tea, whose birth name is Calvin George Scott, was born on September 3, 1959, in the parish of Clarendon. He is a reggae singer and songwriter who began his career as a teenager from the exposure gained by singing in church and school choirs, recording his first song, "Searching in the Hills" in 1974. With no success, he worked as a fisherman and as a race horse jockey for the next five years. He got back into music by working with various sound systems, and in 1983, he moved to Kingston where he met up with top producer Henry 'Junjo' Lawes with whom he recorded his first hit songs "Rocking Dolly" and "I Lost My Sonia". His first album, *Wha Dem A Go Do, Can't Stop Cocoa Tea,* was released in 1985. Over the next three years, he recorded four albums and had a huge hit in

1989 with "Who She Love", a collaboration with dancehall star Shabba Ranks. His career surged in the 90s with hit songs such as "Riker's Island" – which was very popular overseas, "No Blood for Oil" and "Oil Ting" which was banned in Jamaica for its biting social commentary during the Gulf War. Cocoa Tea (so named because of his love for the hot beverage), over his long career, has firmly established himself as one of reggae's most beloved singers. He added the role of promoter to his resume with the staging of the now defunct "Reggae Jam Jam", a large stage show that used to be held on December 31st in Clarendon.

D

MONEY
IN A POCKET
THE DEFINITIVE
COLLECTION

DAMIAN JR.GONG MARLEY
WELCOME TO JAMICA

DennisBrown
THE COMPLETE A&M YEARS

DAMIAN JR.GONG MARLEY
BEAUTIFUL FEATURING BOB BROWN

INCLUDES FREE POSTER!

dennis
brown
UNCHALLENGED

DAMIAN MARLEY
JR.GONG
HALFWAY TREE

GRELCD138 · FEATURES 2 EXTRA CD ONLY TRAC

DAMIAN MARLEY

Damian 'Junior Gong' Marley was born on July 21, 1978, in Kingston. He is a three time Grammy Award winning reggae artiste and is the youngest son of reggae legend Bob Marley. Damian has been performing since the age of 13 and his first album *Mr. Marley* was released in 1996. *Half Way Tree* was next, winning the Grammy Award for Best Reggae Album in 2002. He again won the Grammy Award for best Reggae Album in 2006 for *Welcome to Jamrock* and also Best Urban/Alternative Performance for the title track "Welcome to Jamrock". He has collaborated with international acts such as Snoop Dog, Cyprus Hill and Gwen Stefani. Damian frequently tours with his brothers Julian and Stephen Marley, who are both members of the Ghetto Youths Crew. On September 19, 2006, Damian became the first reggae act to perform for the popular PBS show Austin City Limits. In 2010, he collaborated with American rapper Nas on the critically acclaimed album *Distant Relatives.*

His single, the love-themed "Affairs of the Heart" released in February 2012, was a hit locally and abroad.

As a practicing Rastafarian, Damian Marley's music reflects both his beliefs and the Rastafarian guiding principles of one love, one planet and freedom for all.

DENNIS BROWN

Dennis Emanuel Brown, born February 1, 1957, was a reggae singer and songwriter. He was Bob Marley's favourite singer, and the reggae great dubbed him 'The Crown Prince of Reggae'. Dennis Brown was a prolific artiste, having recorded more than 50 albums and was one of the pioneers of lover's rock, a sub-genre of reggae. Brown's first recording was "Lips of Wine" recorded for Derrick Harriot, but this was not released initially. He then recorded for Coxsone Dodd at the famed Studio One, and Dodd released Brown's first single, "No Man is an Island". Brown recorded two albums for Dodd, *No Man is an Island* and *If I Follow my Heart* (the title track penned by Alton Ellis). Around this time, Brown recorded material for Lloyd Daley ("Baby Don't Do It" and "Things in

Life") and material for Derrick Hariott, which was eventually released as the *Super Reggae and Soul Hits* album. He also worked for Earl Hayles and the Charmaine label early in his career. His first big hit, "Money In My Pocket" on the Joe Gibbs label, was a UK top 20 hit in 1979 (reaching #14 on the singles chart). This led to his contract with A&M Records and by the late 1970s Brown had recorded and performed chart-toppers such as "Sitting & Watching", "Wolves and Leopards", "Here I Come" and "Revolution". As the dancehall era of the 1980s arrived, Brown frequently recorded with King Jammy and Gussie Clark. His song "Revolution" is featured on the reggae radio station K-JAH Radio West in the 2004 video game Grand Theft Auto San Andreas. One of Jamaica's most beloved artistes, he passed away on July 1, 1999 after being rushed to a hospital in Kingston. The official cause of his death was a collapsed lung. His funeral was held on July 17, 1999. He was buried at Kingston's National Heroes Park.

EF

ELEPHANT MAN

Elephant Man, also known as 'The Energy God' due to his energetic and unorthodox live performances, was born O'neil Bryan on September 11, 1975, in Kingston. Elephant Man started out his musical career as a member of the Scare Dem Crew before he later branched out to become a successful solo artiste. He is characterized by several trademarks, such as usually sporting two bright colours in his hair (yellow and orange for e.g.), his stage performances which sometimes include lifting very fat women and dancing with them onstage, and running around and climbing stage props and monitors. His acoustic trademark is a light but distinctive lisp. He is credited for bringing the 'fun' back into dancehall with his slew of dancing hits such as "Pon Di River, Pon Di Bank", the single for which he won the Source Award for Dancehall/Reggae Artiste and a nomination at the 2004 MTV Music Video Awards. His debut album *Good to Go* was released in 2004 on VP records and he was signed to Bad Boy Records as their first ever reggae act with his sophomore album, *Let's Get Physical* released in 2008. Elephant Man frequently collaborates with international acts some of whom include R. Kelly, Swizz Beats, Lil' Jon, Janet Jackson and reggaeton star Daddy Yankee.

He performed at the 2013 BET Awards with Dawn Penn, Beenie Man and Chaka Demus and Pliers to rave reviews.

ETANA

Etana, born Shauna McKenzie in the community of August Town, is a roots reggae singer and songwriter. The only daughter in a large family of boys, she migrated to the United States in 1992. Etana was a bright student and had plans of becoming a registered nurse. However, during her studies at Broward Community College, Etana was bit by the musical bug. In 2000, Etana made a difficult decision. She dropped out of college and joined a female group by the name of Gift. The group, which was being courted by Universal Records, had a sexy and glamorous image which Etana was uncomfortable with. Despite her misgivings, she stuck with it until it was time to shoot the video for their lead single. She reached her limit and walked away from it all, returning to her roots in Kingston,

Jamaica. Etana still wanted to do music but in her own way. In 2005 a friend took her to Fifth Element Records where she auditioned for a shot at becoming a back-up singer for Richie Spice. Etana impressed everyone present and did a few shows in the U.S. Fifteen months later, after stints in Europe and North America, she was ready to make her own mark. Her debut single "Wrong Address", a fusion of jazz and reggae, was an instant hit. Her debut album *Etana The Strong One* was released on VP Records in 2008 and spawned the monster hit single "Warrior Love". Etana's second album, *Free Expression*, was released in 2011 and her third album, *Better Tomorrow*, was released in February 2013.

Regarded by critics as the most promising rising star in reggae music, Etana, through her powerful and captivating voice, and positive lyrics, is poised to take reggae music to higher heights.

GH

gregoryisaacs
Life's Lonely Road

CHARLY

Garnett
Silk
Silky Mood

GARNET

SILK

RULE

DEM

The Roots of the Reggae Messiah

Brand New Me
GREGORY
ISAACS

GREGORY
ISAACS
The Originals

GARNETT
SILK

GIVE I STRENGTH

GARNETT SILK

Garnett Silk, born April 2, 1966, was a reggae musician and singer. His birth name was Garnett Damion Smith and he was born in Greenvale in the cool parish of Manchester. The Rastafarian singer was known for his powerful, yet silky voice. He was one of reggae's rising stars, a singer of rare depth and originality, but his career was ended by his untimely death in 1994. He died while attempting to save his mother during a fire at his home. Silk and his mother were found in each other's arms when their bodies were discovered. Silk's final performance was at the Mirage nightclub where he was part of singer Richie Stephens' birthday celebration on the night before the tragedy took place. He has left behind a superb body of work such as his first big hit "Hello Africa", "Splashing

Dashing", "Kingly Character", "Nothing Can Divide Us" and the seminal album *Its Growing*, hailed by fans and critics alike as a masterpiece of modern roots music.

GREGORY ISAACS

Gregory Anthony Isaacs, born July 15, 1950, in Fletchers Land, Kingston, was a reggae singer and songwriter. In the 1970s, a period which many considered to be his best work, he became one of the most prolific and popular recording artistes in Jamaica, releasing hits such as "My Only Lover", "Sinner Man", "Border", "Number One" and the classic album *Mr. Isaacs* in 1977. Island Records released *Night* Nurse, his best known album, in 1982. The title song was a huge hit and was covered by English pop band Simply Red in 1997 and also by dancehall artiste Lady Saw in 2005. Also known as the 'Cool Ruler', Isaacs had a prominent role in the 1978 film *Rockers* alongside other reggae stalwarts such as Burning Spear and Jacob Miller.

After a long bout with lung cancer, Isaacs died on October 25, 2010, at his home in South London. A memorial service was held on November 20th in Jamaica, which included musical tributes from artistes like Ken Boothe and Freddie McGregor. He was laid to rest at the Dovecot Cemetery.

I WAYNE

I Wayne, born Clifford Taylor in 1980 in Portmore, is a reggae musician that has led the new crop of roots reggae artistes who have burst on the scene over the last several years. In the summer of 2004, I Wayne released "Can't Satisfy Her", a cautionary tale about prostitution and HIV to wide acclaim. The track was the first roots reggae song to be added to the playlist of influential New York radio station, Hot 97. His follow up single, "Living in Love", helped to solidify I Wayne as a consistent hitmaker. His debut album *Lava Ground* was released in 2005 on VP Records.

His sophomore album, *Book of Life* was released in late 2007 and was well received with the singles "Need Her in I Arms" and the title track "Book of Life" garnering significant airplay.

In 2012 he released the single "Love Addiction" and went on a European tour with fellow reggae artiste Fantan Mojah, performing in cities such as Paris, Amsterdam and Munich.

JK

WHY I'M HOT
junior one blood reid

JAH CURE
World Cry
LISTEN
VOICE

JUNIOR
RE

FREE JAH'S CURE
THE ALBUM
THE TRUTH

JUNIOR REID
Big Timer

Jah Cur
TRUE REFLECTION

JAH CURE

Jah Cure, born Siccature Alcock on October 11, 1978, in the parish of Hanover, is a reggae singer and musician. He was given his moniker by reggae star Capleton, whom he met while growing up in Kingston where he was raised. Jah Cure's first big break came in 1997 when he released "King of the Jungle", a duet with Sizzla. The track was produced by Beres Hammond who went on to become his mentor. A steady stream of singles followed, winning him critical and commercial acclaim. In November 1998, while driving around Montego Bay, Jah Cure was pulled over by the police and arrested on charges of gun possession, robbery and rape. He was prosecuted in April 1999, found guilty and sentenced to 15 years in prison. Since the arrest, Jah Cure steadfastly maintained his innocence. While in prison he had access to recording equipment, and released three albums, *Free Jah's Cure: The Album the Truth* in 2000, *Ghetto Life* in 2003, 2005's *Freedom Blues* and a number of singles, some of which topped the Jamaican charts. His popularity soared locally and internationally during his incarceration and he was released from jail on parole on July 28, 2007, after serving 8 years of the 15 year sentence. Three days later, his fourth album, *True Reflections...A New Beginning,* was released. His first concert after he was released took place at the Reggae Sundance Festival in Holland on August 12, 2007.

His 2009 album, *The Universal Cure*, was his first recorded album since his release from prison. *World Cry*, his latest album, has spawned two hit singles, "Unconditional Love" featuring singer Phyllisia and "Like I See It" featuring Mavado and rapper Rick Ross.

JUNIOR REID

Junior Reid, birth name Delroy Reid, was born on June 3, 1965, in Kingston. He is a reggae and dancehall singer and producer. He is best known for the songs "One Blood" and "Funny Man", as well as being the man that replaced Michael Rose as lead vocalist for Black Uhuru. He recorded his first single "Know Myself" at age 14. He then went on to form his own band The Voice of Progress. The group scored a local hit with the single "Mini-Bus Driver" from the album of the same name. By the early 80's, Reid enjoyed considerable popularity with tracks such as "A1 Lover", "Human Nature" and the ghetto anthem "See How Mi Black See How Mi Shine". A capable producer, his JR Production Company and label has worked with artistes such as Elephant Man, Luciano,

Anthony B and the Mighty Diamonds. His recent work with hip hop and R&B artistes introduced Junior Reid to a whole new generation of young hip hop and reggae fans. In 2006 he collaborated with popular California rapper The Game and he was featured on one of the most popular remixes of 2007, the Blackout remix of rapper Mims' "This Is Why I'm Hot". He has also worked with rappers Fat Joe, Jim Jones and Fabolous; and he was featured on a remix version of songstress Alicia Keys' hit single "No One". Reid performed the song alongside Keys at the 2007 American Music Awards.

L

give me the reason

LADY SAW
STRIP TEASE

LUCIANO
RUB-A-DUB
MARKET

lee perry
scratch BACK FROM THE ARK

roots-archives.com
18 CRUCIAL TRACKS

Lee
Scratch
PERRY

Techno
PARTY!

WALK O

LADY SAW

LADY SAW

Lady Saw, birth name Marion Hall, was born on July 12, 1972, in the parish of St. Mary. Known as 'the first Lady of Dancehall', she is the first female deejay to win a Grammy Award and to be certified triple-platinum. She is also the first female deejay to headline shows outside her native Jamaica.

Lady Saw's first successes began in the early 1990s. While gun talk ruled the dancehall, she sang with a heavy dose of sexually explicit lyrics, done from her per-spective as a female. Recording for the local Diamond label, she released early hits like "If Him Lef" and "Stab Out de Meat", which were often met with mixed reaction by audiences. At that time, she also became known for her raucous stage shows, which usually included picking men from the audience (or sometimes her own band members) to pull on stage for simulated sex acts.

Due to her penchant for outspokeness and what was considered vulgarity, she was banned from many events. Male contemporaries of Lady Saw were performing similar lyrics at stage shows, but as a female, Lady Saw endured censorship and even outright banning in some instances. She continued to be outspoken though, and often addressed controversial topics such as unfaithful lovers, female degradation, and safe sex in the wake of the emergence of AIDS (from her single "Condom"). Subsequent hits like "No Long Talking", "Sycamore Tree", and "Find a Good Man" further fueled her success as Jamaica's most prominent female deejay. These also were the first songs to gain exposure in the United States, especially in cities with a large Caribbean diaspora such as New York and Miami.

Lady Saw has collaborated with her male and female peers on several tracks: with Beenie Man on "Healing"; with Sean Paul on "Bossman"; with her protege Ce'Cile on "Loser"; and with long-time friend Tanya Stephens on "Bruck Dem Up". Saw has also worked with international acts such as Missy Elliott, Lil' Kim, Vitamin C and Foxy Brown.

Her 2007 release, *Walk Out,* debuted at number 2 on the Top Reggae Albums chart. The singles "Infertility" and "Chat To Mi Back" were well received. In 2003, Lady Saw received her greatest mainstream honour: she won the Grammy Award for Best Performance by a Duo or Group for her collaboration with pop group No Doubt on the song "Underneath It All".

Her latest album, *My Way,* was released in late 2010. She was crowned 'Queen of the Dancehall' at the 2012 staging of Reggae Sumfest.

LEE SCRATCH PERRY

Lee 'Scratch' Perry, birth name Rainford Hugh Perry, was born on March 20, 1936, in the rural district of Kendal. Perry is a reggae and dub artiste, who has been highly influential in the development and acceptance of reggae and dub music in Jamaica and overseas. He has numerous pseudonyms, such as 'Pipecock Jaxxon' and 'The Upsetter'. Perry's musical career began in the late 1950s as a record seller for Clement Coxsone Dodd's sound system. As his sometimes turbulent relationship with Dodd developed, he found himself performing a variety of important tasks at Dodd's Studio One hit factory, going on to record nearly 30 songs for the label. Disagreements between the pair due to personality and financial conflicts, a recurring theme throughout Perry's career, led him to leave the studio and seek new musical outlets. He soon found a new home at Joe Gibbs' Amalgamated records.

Working with Joe Gibbs, Perry continued his recording career but, once again, financial problems caused conflict. Perry broke ranks with Gibbs and formed his own label, Upsetter, in 1968. His first single "People Funny Boy", which was an insult directed at Gibbs, sold very well. It was notable for its innovative use of a sample (a crying baby) as well as a fast, chugging beat that would soon become identifiable as "reggae" (the new sound did not really have a name at this time). From 1968 until 1972 he worked with his studio band The Upsetters. During the 1970s, Perry released numerous recordings on a variety of record labels that he controlled, and many of his songs were popular in both Jamaica and the UK. He soon became known for his innovative production techniques as well as his eccentric character.

In the early 1970s, Perry was one of the producers whose mixing board experiments resulted in the creation of dub. In 1973, Perry built a studio in his back yard, The Black Ark, to have more control over his productions and continued to produce notable musicians such as Bob Marley & The Wailers, Junior Byles, The Heptones, The Congos and Max Romeo. With his own studio at his disposal, Perry's productions became more lavish, as the energetic producer was able to spend as much time as he wanted on the music he produced. It is important to note that virtually every-thing Perry recorded in The Black Ark was done using rather basic recording equipment, but Perry made it sound unique. Perry remained behind the mixing board for many years, producing songs and albums that stand out as a high point in reggae history.

His modern music is a far cry from his reggae days in Jamaica. Many now see Perry as more of a performance artiste in several respects. In 2003, Perry won a Grammy Award for Best Reggae Album with the album

Jamaican E.T. In 2004, Rolling Stone Magazine ranked Perry #100 on their list of the 100 Greatest Artistes of All Time. More recently, he teamed up with a group of Swiss musicians and performed under the name Lee Perry and the White Belly Rats, and made a brief visit to the United States using the New York City based group Dub Is A Weapon as his backing band. Perry released *Repentance,* a full-length album in 2007. It was co-produced by noted musician Andrew W.K.

Perry resides in Switzerland with his wife Mireille.

LUCIANO

Luciano, born Jepther McClymont, is a roots reggae artiste. Luciano is the seventh of nine children and was born to extremely spiritual and musical parents while growing up in Davey Town, a small district in the central parish of Manchester. Strongly influenced by Stevie Wonder, Frankie Paul and the late, great reggae star Dennis Brown, he first began recording in 1992.

His debut single was "Ebony & Ivory" on the Aquarius Record label and his debut album *Moving Up* was released on RAS records in 1993. In the same year, Luciano scored a #1 song in the UK with the hit "Shake it up Tonight".

After recording several LPs for Fattis Burell's Xterminator label, Luciano did some recording for Island Records before going independent. His album *Jah Words* which featured singles such as the romantic "Angel Heart" and the political "Cry for Justice" was released in 2005.

Luciano is a devout Rastafarian and his music promotes peace, harmony and consciousness, eschewing vulgarity and violence. He has openly criticized other Rastafarian reggae artistes who record vulgar and violent music, describing them as having lost focus.

He has been called a zealot and criticized for reading Biblical verses at the start of his performances, an act deemed inappropriate by many. In 2009, the singer, to the shock of many, was charged by the Jamaican police for harbouring a fugitive who reportedly shot three officers before hiding at Luciano's residence. He was cleared of all charges related to the incident on March 11, 2011.

The award-winning artiste, who has won numerous awards including 'Most Spiritual and Educative Singer' and 'Most

Cultural Artiste', was awarded the Order of Distinction in the rank of officer on October 15, 2007, in recognition of his contribution to the growth of reggae music.

M

NO

Ting a Ling
a Ling a
School
Pickney
Sing Ting

NINJAMAN

Marcia
GRIFFITHS
and friends

MACKA DIAMOND
"Money-O"

ninjaman
ninja is a ninja

MACKA DIAMOND

Macka Diamond,
born Charmaine
Munroe in Kingston,
is a dancehall artiste. She grew up around
music – her father, Phillip Munroe, was a record
producer who has worked with Gregory
Isaacs and was friendly with industry stalwarts
such as King Jammy and the production
duo Sly and Robbie. Her first recording was
the single "Don Girl" on the King Tubby
label under the stage name Lady Mackerel.
She followed up with several recordings
but without achieving the success she
desired, she took some time off from the
business and in 2003, armed with a new name
– Macka Diamond – and a new image and
attitude, she made an immediate impact
with songs like "Done a Ready", "Tek Con"
and "Woman we Name". A collaboration
with fellow dancehall artiste Black-er resulted

in Macka's biggest hit to date, "Bun Him". Not one to rest on her laurels, she wrote a novel, Bun Him, loosely based on the concept of the song by the same name, which was released with much fanfare in late 2007. This was followed by *The Real Gangster's Wife* (2010), *Grown and Sexy* (2011) and *Naughty or Nice* (2012). She has also branched off in film, making an appearance on Jamaica's longest running T.V. show, Royal Palm Estate, and playing the lead role in Redemption in Paradise, a feature film.

In 2004 Macka Diamond, a.k.a. the Money Goddess, became the first female dancehall artiste to be signed to Greensleeves Records.

Her most recent hit song is "Dye Dye", which was released in 2013.

MARCIA GRIFFITHS

Marcia Griffiths, full name Marcia Llyneth Griffiths, was born on November 23, 1949, in Kingston. Also called the 'Queen of Reggae', Griffiths started her career in 1964. From 1970 to 1974 she worked together with Bob Andy in the group Bob and Marcia, on the Harry J label. Between 1974 and 1981 she was a member of the I-Three along with group members Judy Mowatt and Rita Marley, which sang back-up for Bob Marley & The Wailers. Her song "Electric Boogie" made the electric slide, a line dance, an international dance craze. It remains the highest-selling single ever by a female reggae singer.

When Jamaica celebrated its 40th year of independence in 2002, Marcia received the Prime Minister's Award of Excellence.

Marcia Griffiths remains one of Jamaica's most beloved singers and performs regularly at venues all over the world.

NINJAMAN

Ninjaman, birth name Desmond John Ballentine, moved to Kingston from his birthplace of Annotto Bay at the age of 11 and launched his musical career with the Black Culture Sound System at the age of 12. Performing under the moniker 'Double Ugly', he joined the Killamanjaro Sound System in 1980 and got the opportunity to learn from established deejays Super Cat and Early B, releasing his debut single "Uglyman". He soon after changed his name to Ninjaman. In 1987 he recorded and self produced "Protection", a duet with Courtney Melody, which was his first hit single. His hits, particularly those during the period 1989-1992, namely "Murder Dem", "Above the Law" and "Permit to Bury", solidified Ninjaman's image of a violent gangster deejay.

He has had several infamous rivalries with other dancehall stars such as Super Cat, Flourgon and Shabba Ranks in the early nineties, and more recently with Bounty Killer, Merciless and Vybz Kartel, the latter resulting in a physical confrontation on Sting, the world's greatest one night reggae and dancehall show. He has run afoul of the law on several occassions and was sentenced to one year in jail in late 1999 after being convicted of unlawfully possessing a firearm and ammunition. He was incarcerated on a murder charge stemming from the death of a twenty year old man in March 2009. He was denied bail on several occassions until March 2012, when after three years behind bars, he was finally granted bail. Ninjaman is a true dancehall icon and though he doesn't record much in the studio at this stage of his career, he is still relevant and is a staple at many annual shows across the island, when he manages to stay out of jail.

P

TOSH

PETER TOSH

Can't Blam
The Youth

PETER TOSH

PETER TOSH
WANTED

THE BEST OF
PETER TOSH
The Millennium Collec

20th
CENTURY masters

Peter
TOSH

BUSH DOCTOR · JOHNNY B GOODE
NO NUCLEAR WAR · COMING IN HOT
PICK MYSELF UP · EQUAL RIGHTS

GOLD

PETER TOSH

Peter Tosh, born Winston Hubert McIntosh, on October 9, 1944, was the guitarist in the original Wailing Wailers, a reggae musician, and a trailblazer for the Rastafari movement.

Tosh grew up in the ghetto of Trench Town in Kingston. He began to sing and learn guitar at a young age, inspired by the American stations he could pick up on his radio. In the early 1960s Tosh met Bob Marley and Bunny Wailer through his vocal teacher, Joe Higgs.

While perfecting their sound, the trio would often play together on street corners in Trench Town. Joe Higgs was the man who taught the trio to harmonize as well as teaching Marley to play the guitar. In 1962, he was the driving force behind the formation of The Wailing Wailers with Junior Braithwaite and backup singers Beverley Kelso and Cherry Smith. The Wailing Wailers had a huge ska hit with their first single, "Simmer Down", and recorded several more successful singles before Braithwaite, Kelso and Smith left the band in late 1965. Marley spent much of 1966 in America with his mother, Cedella (Malcolm) Marley-Booker and for a short time was working at a nearby Chrysler factory. He then returned to Jamaica in early 1967 with a renewed interest in music and a new spirituality. Tosh and Bunny were already Rastafarians when Marley returned from the U.S., and the three became heavily involved in the Rastafari movement. Soon afterwards, they renamed the group The Wailers.

Tosh began recording under the name Peter Tosh, and released his solo debut, *Legalize It*, in 1976 on CBS Records. The title track soon became an anthem for supporters of marijuana legalization, reggae lovers and Rastafarians all over the world, and was a favourite at Tosh's concerts. Always taking the militant approach, he released *Equal Rights* in 1977.

In 1978, during Bob Marley's free One Love Peace Concert, Tosh lit a marijuana joint and lectured about legalizing marijuana, lambasting Prime Minister Michael Manley and Opposition Leader Edward Seaga for their failure to enact such legislation.

Several months later, he was apprehended by the police in Kingston and was severely beaten while in police custody.

Tosh put together a backing band, Word, Sound and Power, who were to accompany him on tour for the next few years, and the band appeared on his albums of this period. In 1978 Rolling Stones Records signed Tosh, and the album *Bush Doctor* was released, introducing Tosh to a larger audience. The single from the album, a cover of The Temptations song "Don't Look Back", performed as a duet with Rolling Stones singer Mick Jagger, turned Tosh into one of the best known reggae artistes.

After an illustrious career with The Wailers and as a solo musician, he was murdered at his home on September 11, 1987. Robbery was officially said to be the motivation behind his death.

S

mr. loverman

Featuring Jack Radio

SUPER CAT
MY GIRL JOSEPHINE

TAKEN FROM
THE ALBUM
PRET
PORTER

shaggy
IT WASN'T ME
FEATURING RIKROK

SHABBA
RANKS

X-TRA
NAKED

SIZZLA

GHETTO
REVOLUTION

sean pa
temperature

SEAN PAUL

Sean Paul, birth name Sean Paul Ryan Frances Henriques, was born January 8, 1973 in Canada. Both his parents are Jamaicans and he grew up in an affluent neighbourhood in St. Andrew, Jamaica. Coming from a family of swimmers, Sean Paul competed for the national water polo team from age thirteen to twenty-one. However, dancehall music was his first love, and he gave up the sport to launch his musical career. In 1996, Sean Paul released his debut single "Baby Girl (Don't Cry)" with producer Jeremy Harding. It proved to be a success and led to other hits such as "Deport Them", "Infiltrate" and "Nah Get Nuh Bly (One More Try)". In 1999, Sean Paul made strides on the international scene when his collaboration with fellow dancehall artiste Mr. Vegas "Top Shotta"

was included in the film Belly. That year, he also scored a top ten hit on the billboard hip hop charts with "Hot Gal Today". His debut album *Stage One* was released in March 2000 on VP Records. It included many of his previous hit singles and compilation cuts, plus several new tracks. In 2002, he released his second album, *Dutty Rock.* It was a worldwide success, eventually selling over six million copies and won the Grammy Award for Best Reggae Album. The videos for the monster hit singles "Gimme the Light" and "Get Busy" were staples on music channels like MTV and BET, and catapulted Sean Paul into stardom. Several high profile collaborations, including "Baby Boy" with Beyonce and "Breathe" with Blu Cantrell further solidified his reputation as a prominent hitmaker. 2005's *The Trinity,* his third album, also went platinum and spawned the hits "We Be Burnin'", "Temperature" and "Never Gonna Be the Same". His fourth album, *Imperial Blaze,* was released in August 2009.

Tomahawk Technique, his fifth album, was released in Europe and Japan in March 2012, and the first single "Got 2 Luv U" went number one in Spain and Germany. The album has made the top-10 charts in France, Austria and Switzerland.

SHABBA RANKS

Shabba Ranks, birth name Rexton Rawlston Fernando Gordon, was born on January 17, 1966, in the parish of St. Ann. He stands among the most popular dancehall artistes of his generation and was one of the first dancehall acts to gain acceptance worldwide. When he was eight years old, his family moved to the ghetto of Trench Town, in Kingston. By age 12, he was fascinated by the sound system DJs who spun records in local clubs, and often chatted on the microphone over the backing tracks. Some of his early inspirations were Brigadier Jerry, Charlie Chaplain and Josey Wales. He initially called himself Co-Pilot and his first single, "Heat Under Sufferer's Feet" was released in 1985. It caught the ear of his idol Josey Wales, who took the young artiste under his wing and introduced him to some of the producers at King Jammy's studio. He recorded the single "Original Fresh" and a host of other singles, none of which gave him a break-through hit. In 1988, he released the single "Needle Eye Punany", which marked the beginning of his notorious sexual explicitness and which made him extremely popular in Jamaica. The pivotal move in his career and the one which propelled him into stardom, was his move to former King Jammy's engineer/producer Bobby Digital's new studio and label, Digital B. The duo's chemistry was immediate and between 1989-1991 Shabba recorded some 50 singles, mainly with Bobby Digital but also with producers Steely & Clevie, and Gussie Clarke. The barrage of hits included "Live Blanket", "Maama Man", "Wicked in Bed" and "Roots and Culture". Smash hit singles such as "Telephone Love", a duet with J.C. Lodge, and "Twice my Age", a duet with Krystal, were extremely popular overseas, particularly in the UK. Major record label, Epic Records, took notice and signed Shabba to a deal in 1991. His Epic debut, *As Raw as Ever,* was a huge crossover hit and Shabba became the first dancehall artiste to win a Grammy Award for Best Reggae Album. His follow-up album, *X-tra Naked*, was also a big hit, and won Shabba back to back Grammy Awards for Best Reggae Album. His 1994 single, "Family Affair", was a hit off the Addams Family Values soundtrack. His 1995 album, *A Mi Shabba* had some minor hit singles such as "Shine Eye Gal" and "Let's Get It On" but the album was not as successful as its predecessors. Shabba lives in New York City and still records and performs periodically. He appeared on a track called "Clear the Air" by Busta Rhymes & Akon in 2007, and he released a single "None a Dem" in 2011 which received significant airplay in Jamaica.

Shabba, after not performing in Jamaica for over a decade, made a triumphant return at the 2012 staging of Reggae Sumfest, where he performed on International Night.

SHAGGY

Shaggy, birth name Orville Richard Burrell, was born on October 22, 1968, in Kingston. His family moved to the United States and they settled in the neighbourhood of Flatbush, Brooklyn. In 1988 he joined the United States Marine Corps and while enlisted, he served during Operation Desert Storm during the Persian Gulf War. Upon his return from the Persian Gulf, he decided to pursue a career in music. He had his first hit in 1993, "Oh Carolina", a dancehall re-make of a ska hit by the Folkes Brothers. Another massive hit for him was *Boombastic* in 1995 for which he won the Grammy Award for Best Reggae Album. The title track, "Boombastic", was used as the theme tune in a popular Levi's commercial. He took the world by storm with 2001's diamond selling (over 10 million copies sold) album *Hot Shot* which spawned two worldwide number 1 singles "It Wasn't Me" and "Angel". The album itself would hit number one on the Billboard 200 chart. He was unable to replicate the success of *Hot Shot* with the release of his next two albums, 2002's *Lucky Day*, and *Clothes Drop*, released in 2005. Another album, *Intoxication*, was released in 2007 and had a hit single "Church Heathen". In April 2008, Shaggy was selected to record the official anthem for the mascots of the Euro 2008 football tournament. The song "Feel The Rush", topped the charts in most of Europe. His 2009 single, "Bad Man No Cry", received significant airplay on the Jamaican airwaves. On July 16, 2011 he launched a new album, *Summer in Kingston* and the lead single, "Sugar Cane", has done well on itunes.

He created the Shaggy Make a Difference Foundation to help raise funds for the Bustamante Hospital for Children in Kingston.

SIZZLA KALONJI

Sizzla Kalonji, or simply **Sizzla**, was born Miguel Orlando Collins on April 17, 1976, in St. Mary. Sizzla, an accomplished singer and songwriter, subscribes to the Bobo Ashanti branch of the Rastafari movement.

Sizzla began to develop his own style whilst serving his musical apprenticeship with the Caveman Hi-Fi sound system. He kickstarted his recording career in 1995 with a release through the Zagalou label and then teamed up with 'Bobby Digital' Dixon for a series of singles. Extensive touring with fellow roots and culture artiste Luciano followed, earning Sizzla notability.

Jermaine Fagan, the same man who gave Buju Banton his first break, introduced Sizzla to top Jamaican saxophonist Dean Fraser, the musical director for Philip 'Fatis'

Burrell's Xterminator Family. 1996 marked an important turning point for Sizzla when he began working with Fatis. This union led to a run of successful singles and the release of Sizzla's debut album, *Burning U.*

The two collaborated again a year later with the follow-up, *Praise Ye Jah* (JetStar). *Praise Ye Jah* was quickly trumped by his release of the Dixon-produced *Black Woman & Child* that same year. The title track was a smash hit and became something of a cultural reggae anthem. Sizzla scored several more hits during 1997, including "Like Mountain", "Babylon Cowboy", "Kings of the Earth", and the Luciano duet "Build a Better World".

Along with universal praise came Sizzla's first nomination for Best International Reggae Artiste of the Year at the 1998 MOBO Awards and a place in various magazines' top 100 albums of the year. Sizzla has since released several dozen albums, including 1998's *Kalonji* and *Royal Son of Ethiopia* in 1999. That year also saw him receive his second MOBO nomination. Sizzla has 21 albums that have made it onto the Billboard's Top Reggae Albums music chart, the highest, *Words of Truth*, reaching the position of #5.

He has started his own record company, Kalonji Records; which in a joint venture with Damon Dash Music Group and Koch Records, released the album, *The Overstanding*, in November 2006. This was his third album released through Kalonji Records; as well as *Black History* and *Life*.

In 2004, Sizzla was barred from entering the UK for several concerts and was among a group of reggae artistes who were being investigated by Scotland Yard for allegedly inciting murder through their lyrics. Multiple songs contain anti-gay lyrics, as many followers of the Rastafarian Movement oppose homosexuality. In 2007, Sizzla's concerts in Toronto and Montreal were cancelled after protests from Canada's gay rights groups. He released the album *Ghetto Youth-ology* in 2008.

After a brief hiatus from the music scene due to injuries sustained in a motor vehicle accident, Sizzla's career has seen a resurgence in late 2012. His superb performance at the Sir Arthur Guiness celebration concert in September, was followed by an intimate, extremely well-received set at Usain Bolt's Tracks and Records Behind the Scenes series in early October.

Judgement Yard was established as a community centre in August Town by Sizzla Kalonji. He maintains one of his residences there and Judgement Yard is also the home of Kalonji's state of the art studio, as well as his record label, Kalonji Records.

SUPER CAT

Super Cat, birth name William Maragh, was born in Kingston in 1963. He is one of the originators of the late 80's and early 90's dancehall movement. Super Cat is of Indian descent and his nick-name the 'Wild Apache' was given to him by his mentor, Early B. Super Cat was raised in Kingston's tough Seivright Gardens neighbourhood, then known as Cockburn Pen.

The community was a hotbed of dance-hall and home to ground-breaking deejays like Prince Jazzbo and U-Roy. As a child, Super Cat heard the latest songs by these veterans blasting from local record shops. By the time he was eight years old, he was hanging out at a local club called Bamboo

Lawn, assisting the crew of the Soul Imperial sound system and absorbing the dancehall rhymes of deejays like Dillinger, Ranking Trevor and Early B The Doctor.

His first single, released in 1981, was entitled "Mr. Walker" and was a hit in Jamaica. His song "Boops" came soon after with the release of his debut album *Si Boops Deh* and was a massive hit.

Super Cat had a number of hit singles in the early 1990s, including "Don Dada", "Ghetto Red Hot" and "Dem No Worry We" with Heavy D. In 1992, he was featured on the remix of "Jump" with Kris Kross, and he also collaborated with them in 1993 for their song "It's Alright".

These hits made him The Source Magazine dancehall artiste of the year in 1993. He was also an early collaborator with The Notorious B.I.G., featuring the then unknown artiste (along with Mary J. Blige, Jesse West and Puff Daddy) on the B-side remix of "Dolly My Baby" in 1993.

Super Cat was featured on the number one hit "Fly", a 1997 single by Sugar Ray from their platinum album. He collaborated with India Arie on her hit song "Video" in 2001, and with Jadakiss and The Neptunes on "The Don Of Dons" in 2003. Also in 2003, he collaborated with 112 for their song "Na, Na, Na".

Following the death of his long time road manager Fred 'The Thunder' Donner in 2004, Super Cat released a multi-cd tribute album entitled *Reggaematic Diamond All-Stars* that featured contributions from Yami Bolo, Michael Prophet, Linval Thompson, Nadine Sutherland and Sizzla among others.

Super Cat treated fans to a rare performance, appearing on a 2008 show at Madison Square Gardens that also featured Buju Banton and Barrington Levy. He also appeared on the Best of the Best concert in Miami that same year.

Super Cat is featured on hip hop star Nas' single "The Don (No DJ)" off Nas' 2012 album *Life is Good*.

A true dancehall legend, Super Cat still has maximum respect from fans and artistes alike.

T

TANYA
STEPHENS
»INFALLIBLE«

TARRUS
RILEY
Parables
implies story illustrating
a moral or religious lesson

THiRd WORLd

J-MAN

TANYA STEPHENS
Gangsta
Blues

TARRUS RILEY
CONTAGIOUS

THiRd WORLd
ROCK THE WORLD

TANYA STEPHENS

Tanya Stephens, birth name Vivienne Stephenson, born on July 2, 1973 in the parish of St. Mary, is a reggae and dancehall artiste. In a male dominated industry dotted with a few females, Stephens has made her mark, introducing an uncommon element of creativity that has earned her international recognition as a one of a kind artiste. Versatile and extremely talented, she seamlessly blends biting social commentary, relationships and partying in her music. She emerged in the late 1990s and her biggest hit to date "Yuh Nuh Ready Fi Dis Yet" was featured on the Reggae Gold 1997 compilation album. She has recorded seven albums, and the former two, 2004's brilliant *Gangsta Blues* which spawned the hit single "It's A Pity" and 2006's uncompromising *Rebelution* which gave us the hit single "These Streets" is tangible proof that Tanya Stephens is one of the brightest musical sparks of her generation.

Fed up with label politics and anxious for her fans to hear her music, her seventh album, *Infallible*, was released in 2010 on the internet for free.

TARRUS RILEY

Tarrus Riley is a roots reggae singer and one of the most promising reggae artistes to emerge on the scene in recent years. He is the son of Jimmy Riley who has had a stellar career as a solo artiste as well as being a former member of The Uniques and The Techniques. Riley taught himself to play keyboards and several percussion instruments such as Kette and Congo, and began writing his own songs, many of which had strong Rastafarian and conscious themes. His first album, *Challenges,* was produced by Dean Fraser, the legendary saxophonist, and spawned the hits "Larger Than Life" and "Barber Chair". *Parables,* his sophomore album, was also produced by Dean Fraser (he produced 14 of the 15 tracks) and featured the legendary rhythm section of Sly Dunbar and Robbie Shakespeare. The album spawned a monster hit in "She's Royal" and other stand out tracks include "Lion Paw" and the title track "Parables". His third album, *Contagious*, was released in 2010.

Riley, who describes his music as 'healing music', has done several concert appearances with his father.

THIRD WORLD

Third World is one of the greatest reggae bands of all time, and was one of Jamaica's most consistently popular crossover acts among international audiences. Third World was originally formed in 1973 by keyboardist Michael 'Ibo' Cooper and guitarist/cellist Steven 'Cat' Coore. Both joined the original lineup of Inner Circle around 1968 and left to form their own band in 1973. The band's debut single, "Railroad Track", was released on the Island label in 1974 and they were the opening act for Bob Marley & the Wailers' European tour that same year. Their self-titled debut album was released in 1976 and featured a successful cover of the Abyssinians' roots classic "Satta Massagana". The follow-up, 1977's *96° in the Shade*, introduced new drummer Willie "Roots" Stewart and new lead singer William Clarke, aka Bunny Rugs. It was an enormous critical success in the U.K. and Europe, and spawned an all-time classic single in the title track. That set the stage for the group's commercial break-through album, 1978's *Journey to Addis*, which featured a funky, disco-flavored reggae cover of the O'Jays' "Now That We Found Love". The song hit the Top Ten on the American R&B charts in 1979, as well as the British pop Top Ten, and the album climbed into the R&B Top 20. The follow-up single, "Cool Meditation", made the British Top 20, and Third World became international stars.

The band's success continued on through the '80s, as 1983's *All the Way Strong* and 1985's *Sense of Purpose* both made the R&B Top 50. The latter album produced several minor crossover hits in the title track, "One on One," and "One More Time," which sported state-of-the-art, club-friendly dance beats.

However, 1987's *Hold on to Love* didn't fare so well, and the group wound up parting ways with CBS and moving over to Mercury. Their 1989 label debut, *Serious Business*, restored their commercial standing with American R&B audiences, climbing into the Top 30 on the strength of a third major crossover hit, "Forbidden Love". One of the first commercially successful fusions of reggae and rap, "Forbidden Love" featured a guest appearance by Stetsasonic lead rapper Daddy O, and charted in the R&B Top 20. *Serious Business* also marked the departure of Irvin "Carrot" Jarrett, who was briefly replaced by "Forbidden Love" co-writer Rupert 'Gypsy' Bent III.

Third World's second Mercury album was 1992's dancehall-flavored *Committed*, which produced a Top 30 R&B hit in the title cut. However, it proved to be their last major-label outing. Their next release, 1994's concert set *Live It Up*, appeared on the band's own label and marked the return of Rupert Bent, who wound up joining the band as a guitarist, keyboardist, percussionist, and occasional vocalist. In 1997, founding member Michael 'Ibo' Cooper and Willie Stewart both departed, and were replaced by keyboardist Leroy 'Baarbe' Romans and drummer Tony 'Ruption' Williams, respectively. This lineup released *Generation Coming* in 1999, landing guest spots from Shaggy and Bounty Killer. Afterwards, Romans was replaced by Herbie Harris, who made his studio debut on 2003's *Ain't Givin' Up*.

That same year the band celebrated a quarter century of playing music by re-recording their classics for their 25th Anniversary. Two years later they returned with *Black Gold and Green* which included guests Beres Hammond, Wayne Marshall, and Blu Fox.

V

VYBZ KARTEL
LYRICIST

VYBZ KARTEL
THE TEACHER'S BACK

VYBZ KARTEL
PON DI GAZA *Mi Say*

VYBZ KARTEL
Summer Tim

VYBZ KARTEL
Clarks DE MIX TAPE
RAW

VYBZ KARTEL
Up 2 Di Time

MIXED BY DJ WAYNE

PARENTAL ADVISORY
EXPLICIT CONTENT

VYBZ KARTEL

Vybz Kartel, born Adidja Palmer in Waterhouse, Kingston, is the most controversial, and arguably, the most lyrically gifted dancehall artiste. He grew up in the Waterford community of Portmore and attended Calabar high school from which he was expelled.

Determined to finish his education, he completed his studies at a technical school. Vybz Kartel was exposed to a wide variety of music at an early age by an uncle who was a disc jockey, ranging from country & western to reggae. Young Adidja would write down the lyrics to his favourite songs, study them and perform them to entertain his friends.

Deciding he wanted to be a deejay, he began writing his own lyrics at age 11. In 1996, Adidja formed a group with two of his friends and named it Vybz Cartel. However, the group was short-lived and Adidja changed the spelling of Cartel to Kartel and pursued a solo career as Vybz Kartel.

His career took off when he was introduced to ace DJ Bounty Killer and the two immediately clicked. He began penning lyrics for Bounty Killer and was one of the artistes in Bounty Killer's crew called the Alliance. He came into his own with hits like "Sweet To The Belly"; "New Millennium" and "Why You Doing It" (done in collaboration with Wayne Marshall); "Tek Buddy Gal" – one of his most controversial hits and "Sen On" done with Canadian rapper Kardinal Official.

Lyrical battles with the likes of Assassin, Spragga Benz, a physical as well as lyrical war with Ninja Man, and an acrimonous parting from the Alliance which resulted in a longstanding feud with Mavado, has helped solidify the street credibility of this talented, hardcore entertainer. After leaving the Alliance he formed his own crew of up and coming artistes called the Portmore Empire. Also known as 'Addi de Teacha', 'World Boss' and 'Gaza Emperor', Vybz Kartel has been a major force to be reckoned with since 2003, and shows no sign of letting up on his dominance of dancehall.

The highly intelligent and articulate lyricist is at the top of his game, dropping hit after hit, such as 2009's "Ramping Shop" which debuted on the Billboard top 100 singles chart and "Clarks" which was featured on the TV series So You Think You Can Dance Canada and was one of the top 3 reggae/dancehall singles gaining airplay in North America for 40 weeks.

In 2010 he released the album *Pon Di Gaza 2.0* on his own label Adidjahiem/Notnice Records in collaboration with distributor Tads Records and 2011 saw the release of the impressive album *Kingston Story*, produced by famed hip hop/electro producer Dre Skull. His catchy 2011 single, "Summertime", was the most popular dancehall track for the summer in Jamaica.

Quite the entrepreneur, Vybz Kartel has his own liquor – Street Vybz Rum, condoms, soap, and plans are underfoot for his own line of sneakers. He also used to be part owner of a nightclub, until a very public split with his business partner.

Always embroiled in controversy, his noticably lighter complexion due to skin bleaching was and still is a huge topic of discussion in Jamaica as well as among the diaspora. His detractors condemned him for trying to look white while his loyal fans mostly stated that they did not care what he looked like.

Kartel, who is a master at turning controversy into profit, came out with a line of 'cake soap' which he had initially insisted was the source of his lighter complexion, and also had plans for a line of skin care products and a unisex fragrance called 'Oh!', named after one of his signature phrases. His highly anticipated reality show Teacher's Pet, where 20 women vie for his affection, debuted in September 2011 and was the most watched show in the history of the network.

His business ventures and penchant for controversy not withstanding, the music is the foundation of his brand, and Vybz Kartel's lyrical prowess has not gone unnoticed internationally. He has collaborated with the likes of Sean Kingston, Rihanna, Heather Headley, Missy Elliot, Ghostface Killah, Mims, Jim Jones, Nina Sky and Juelz Santana.

His illustrious career was dealt a blow when he was arrested and charged with murder, conspiracy to murder and illegal possession of a firearm on September 29,

2011. He was granted bail on one murder charge but currently remains in jail on a second murder charge.

He maintains his innocence and fans worldwide are hoping that he will soon be set free.

XYZ

A Very, Very
Yellow Christmas
RAS RECORDS

Yellowman

YELLOWMAN
MOST WANTED

YELLOWMAN

Yellowman, born Winston Foster in Negril, in 1959, is a reggae and dancehall icon. He was popular in Jamaica in the 1980s, coming to prominence with a series of singles that established his reputation.

Graphic sexuality was his main forte, and the sexual explicitness in his music was a huge part of his appeal and popularity despite his numerous detractors.

However, his lyrical content was not the only reason for his popularity. Yellowman was very talented, blessed with wit, a sublime delivery and a knack for improvisation.

Yellowman grew up at the Maxfield Park Children's Home and the Alpha Boys Home respectively in Kingston, and was shunned due to having albinism, which was usually not socially accepted in Jamaica.

In the late 1970s Yellowman first gained wide attention when he won a talent contest in Kingston. Like many local DJs, he honed his talents by frequently performing at outdoor sound system dances. In 1981, after establishing his name in Jamaica, Yellowman became the first dancehall artiste to be signed to a major American label (CBS Records). His first album, *Mister Yellowman*, was released in 1982, bringing him instant success. It was followed by *Zungguzungguguzungguzeng* in 1983.

Yellowman has had a substantial influence on the world of hip hop. He is widely credited for leading the way for the succession of dancehall artistes that were embraced by the growing hip hop community in America during the 80s. He became Jamaica's most popular dancehall act despite being an albino. During the early 1980s, Yellowman had over 40 singles and produced up to 5 albums a year.

In 1986, he struggled with cancer of the jaw and doctors only gave him six months to live. However, he underwent surgery that saved his life. Yellowman often used sexually explicit lyrics in his songs, boasting of his sexual prowess, but the near brush with death gave him a more serious approach to his music. He took an extended leave from recording due to his health but came back strong with *Blueberry Hill.* He re-invented himself with 1994's *Prayer*, and since the mid-90s, he has devoted his time to spiritual and social concerns.

His latest albums are 2003's *New York* and *Round 1* in 2005. He was also a guest artiste on the Run-DMC track "Roots Rap Reggae". Yellowman is one of the widest-touring artistes in the reggae industry, routinely performing in places such as Peru, France, Italy and Germany.

TEN TIMELESS REGGAE AND DANCEHALL ALBUMS

Exodus by Bob Marley & The Wailers: In  1999, Time Magazine voted *Exodus* the most important album of the 20th century. Recorded in London after an attempt on his life, *Exodus* showcases a mellower, more reflective Marley. While there are some powerful political tracks on the album, Marley adopts a less fiery approach than his previous recordings. The results were spectacular, spawning timeless poetic love songs such as "Turn Your Lights Down Low" and huge international hits like "Waiting in Vain", "Jamming" and "One Love/People Get Ready".

Exodus is indeed a musical masterpiece that has withstood the test of time.

Half Way Tree by Damian 'Junior Gong'

Marley: One of the best modern reggae albums ever recorded, the Grammy Award winning *Half Way Tree* successfully bridges the gap between several disparate musical sounds. Rapper Eve appears on the funky "Where is the Love?", dancehall star Capleton shows up on the brilliant "It Was Written" and his brother Stephen, who was the executive producer of the album, graces "Catch a Fire" with his silky harmonies as the brothers admirably update their father's (Bob Marley) classic "Slave Driver".

Til Shiloh by Buju Banton: A must have for anyone who truly loves reggae music, *Til Shiloh* is by far Buju Banton's best and most personal work. Banton reflects on the

world in which we live on the haunting sufferer's gem "Untold Stories", paid homage to the motherland on "Til I'm Laid to Rest" and struggles with his grief and desire for vengeance in coping with the murders of two close friends on the powerful and emotionally raw "Murderer". Banton goes on a spiritual and emotional journey with this album, and he effectively carries the listener along with him for the entire ride.

As Raw as Ever by Shabba Ranks: A

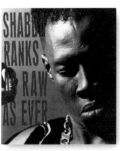

very good, energetic set by one of Jamaica's first break out dancehall stars, this 1991 recording is hard-edged, abrasive and tough. Featuring cross-over hits like the Maxi Priest duet "House

Call" and the KRS-ONE rap collaboration "The Jam" and gems such as "Trailer Load a Girls", fast forward twenty-one years and this album is still pleasing to the ears.

Hot Shot by Shaggy: Shaggy successfully  bridges the gap between commercially successful pop and reggae music on this diamond selling 2001 release. With huge worldwide number one singles such as "Angel" and "It Wasn't Me", and talented guest vocalists who complement his personality on each track, *Hot Shot* is a humorous, fun and musically pleasing listen.

Mama Africa by Peter Tosh: Originally released in 1983, *Mama Africa* is easily Tosh's most "accessible" body of work and the only one of his solo releases to break into the UK top 50. Every track is memorable in its own way, as Tosh combines styles,

moods and genres across songs old and new. Containing covers such as the chart topping "Johnny B. Goode" and "Stop That Train"; and hits such as the spiritual "Glasshouse" and the Pan-African title track "Mama Africa", which shows Peter Tosh approaching the zenith of his career.

Don Dada by Super Cat: The best album from one of dancehall's first real stars. It spawned the hits "Dem Nuh Worry We" which featured rapper Heavy D, "Ghetto Red Hot", "Nuff Man a Dead" and the boastful title track "Don Dada". A must have for any true dancehall fan.

Mister Yellowman by Yellowman:

 Originally released in 1982, this is the best album from an impressive catalogue belonging to the first dancehall artiste to be signed to a major label. From the romantic "Yellowman Getting Married" to the humorous "Cocky Did a Hurt Me" to the sexual "Morning Ride", *Mister Yellowman* is classic dancehall at its best.

Legend by Bob Marley: The crème de  la crème as far as compilation albums go, *Legend* featuring gems like "I Shot the Sheriff" and "No Woman No Cry" provides an accurate insight into the musical genius of Bob Marley. *Legend* has sold over 20 million copies worldwide.

TITANIA'S WISHING SPELLS

PEACE
TITANIA HARDIE

QUADRILLE

As I write, we are living through times of uncertainty, and peace is very much on our minds. We may question what the term means to us: peace between countries, peace of mind, domestic peace, inner peace, concord with friends and family. Also a willingness to be more peaceable and less aggressive amongst ourselves, in the world we inhabit daily. It has never been more important to create a space of personal peace and tranquillity than it is at present. Our domestic world must offer us some sense of inner sanctum to counter the stresses of everyday life.

It would be foolish to promise that magic alone can achieve a total result. However, I do believe that many minds working cheerfully toward peaceful thought and harmony, even individually, can make a difference. It requires a more active feeling of tolerance, understanding, and questioning any degree of dogmatism. We are willing to be approachable, and to meet others – especially loved ones – half way. We also need to maintain our personal feeling of calm most strongly when others around us are ruffled.

These wishing spells draw on the spectacular energy of what my grandmother and mother call 'the wish power'. Put simply, anything you really wish for you can attract – so be careful what you wish for, because it will come true! If you can muster a child-like heart, great determination and cheerful energy, you can make your wishes count – on a personal and on a global scale. The mind has resources and strengths that we haven't fully tried. Here is our chance to wish – all together – for a more peaceful future, both individually and internationally. Let's wish hard…

Blessed Be!

Titania Hardie

APPLE BLOSSOM

The first branch of apple blossom was sometimes
brought into the home and laid near a window
if there had been bad luck or sickness in the house
or among the family. If you have access to an apple
tree, you can partake of this lovely practice.

Bringing in the branch of blossom, ask the goddess of love
and joys to bathe your home in warm rays of peace and
happiness following the darker days you've just endured.
Light an apple-coloured candle to her, and speak her name
in the way you prefer – Aphrodite or Pomona are appropriate.
Keep at least one tiny flower as it withers and place it in
a bowl of pot-pourri, or glue it to a tiny card. Return the
remainder of the branch to the outside world. You should
now experience a period of peace and restfulness.

CHAMBER POT

This is a strange one. Once perhaps the most essential gift for a new house or a newly married couple, the chamber pot was also connected with a great deal of ritual. If you happen upon one in an antiques shop or fair, this is what you may do with it. Otherwise, a bucket would substitute very well.

To ensure peace in a marriage, or a peaceful dwelling place, take a chamber pot (or bucket) to the home, filling it first with salt and some flowers. Jump over the blooming vessel three times, wishing out loud each time – firstly for health, secondly for peace and lastly for prosperity, for this abode and for those living there. The chamber pot can now be used as an indoor plant holder for a shrub that will blossom, but retain some of the salt for magical 'peace and plenty'.

BAY LEAF

Even Pliny attested to the protective powers of the
bay or laurel leaf: it was said to be particularly good
at keeping away thunder and preventing harm from
lightning. There is also a ritual to perform with a bay
leaf in times of civil strife.

If there is talk of war or strife, you must go and pick a bay
leaf in the last hour of light on the day that you heard the news
of trouble. As you pick the leaf, make a wish to the powers
of divinity for a swift resolution. Then take the leaf and pin it
to your shirt or coat, close your eyes and wish for protection
around those closest to you, and friends. Wish that events may
quickly go off the boil, and that peace may soon be regained.
At night, pin the leaf to some fabric near your bed, and note
the message of your dreams.

PIE

Whenever you find you have cut a pie or a cake into three pieces, here is what you should do.

"I wish for me, and I wish for thee, and I wish for the wide world too." Say this and, as you do, make first a wish for peace for yourself (considering the peaceful settling of any arguments). Then make a wish for your guest/s, wishing an end to their troubles. Finally, make a wish to see difficulties between nations settled. Only now can you eat the pie, but save a little of the crust for luck.

Rainbow and straw

This is one of the luckiest tokens of the skies. The gods seem to be sending a sign of promise to those of us below. Straw has also been associated with powerful protection.

When you see a rainbow during a time of difficulty and discord, you should look for a piece of straw or brownish grass on the ground. Hold it up to the rainbow and ask the messenger of the skies to cut your woes in half with a blade of grass. Kiss the grass or straw and put it in your pocket. Blow a huge kiss to the rainbow and put your problems up in the sky beside it. During the next few days, with the first light rainfall, your luck will turn and peace will surround you.

STONE WITH A HOLE

This is not as unusual as it may sound. It is possible to find many stones that naturally have a little hole; if not, there are many huge standing stones that have holes deliberately made within them. These are very lucky indeed, having a strong connection with earth fertility.

Whenever you find or visit such a stone, place a kiss in the hole and close your eyes. Promise three things: to be kind, to be wise and to concentrate on whatever work you are trying to complete until it is done. If you can keep your promise for one lunar month, you will have thirteen moons of luck and peace in your love and home lives.

BLUE BEADS

Blue was associated with the Virgin Mary, but is also the colour of the sky, and thus suggests heavenly intervention. This little ritual is timely if you have just come through a loss in the family, or the end of a relationship.

Ask someone to give you a little gift of some blue beads, or a blue ribbon. Tie them around you (usually your neck) and bow your head quietly, imagining a new peaceful blue light infusing you from head to toe. Keep the blue talisman in place around your neck for at least one week, then it can be moved to a bag, or purse, or even inside a pillow. Your luck will change and peace will replace anxiety and stress.

BIRCH TREES

These are among the luckiest trees you can grow in your garden. Many are the rituals with birch trees, and the leaves are dedicated to protection from witches! They also have a long connection with protection and peaceful deeds.

If you have lost your feelings of personal peace, or have had a quarrel with your lover, you need to find a birch tree. Stand under the tree with your fingers crossed, and close your eyes. Imagine a greeny-yellow light entering your head and heart, making you feel serene and strong again. Speak words of a wish for peace in your life, or between you and someone else. Bow to the tree, uncross your fingers and continue on your way, making your day as busy and distracted as you can.

Matters should improve within three days.

MYRTLE

Myrtle has long been carried in bridal bouquets because of its association with luck in love and marriage. It is also a tree of peace.

Carry out this ritual when you move into a new home, or in with a new love. On the first new moon that occurs after you have moved in, plant a pair of myrtle trees on either side of the front door (they will grow happily in large pots). Place a white feather in the bottom, around the roots. Make a wish-prayer for peace and steady joy in the house and with your partner, and tend the plants regularly with love and respect. While they thrive, so will your peaceful prosperity together.

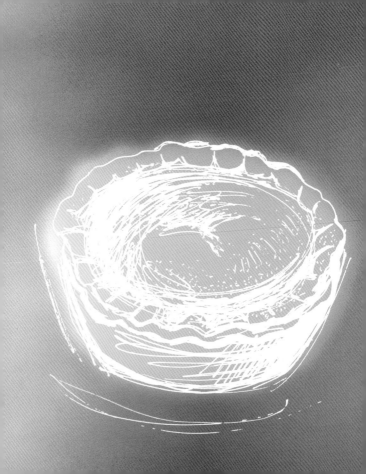

MINCE PIE

The humble mince pie was traditionally regarded
as a distilled drop of fertility and magic in miniature.
Here's what to do with the very first mince pie of
the season.

Serve the first mince pie with a small alcoholic drink, such
as sherry or a cup of brandied coffee. A pot of tea will not do.
Make sure you have at least one friend to share your repast,
and as you bite into the pie, make a wish together. If you wish
for a peaceful Christmas – an unselfish wish that affects all
who come to your home – your wish will be granted.

Fishing

Fishing has some sacred responsibilities attached to it. If you are due to make a fishing trip, follow this advice in order to catch more than your dinner.

First, cut a slit in the wooden handle-tip of the rod, and into this squeeze a silver coin. This action will ensure a good catch overall; but set aside the first fish caught in this way to eat with friends, and dedicate it to a peaceable relationship between you all.

If you are finding it particularly difficult to re-establish a sense of inner peace after a personal crisis, get a friend to take you fishing at the first opportunity. Remember to place the coin in the rod and eat the first fish together, dedicating it to personal peace. You will be amazed by what follows.

Candle

A bright spark seen in the candle flame is a sure sign of a letter. If you have a candle burning and notice a brightly glowing tip – like a red hot-spot – make a wish.

Look into the poker-red spot on the candle wick and wish for a lessening of your sorrows, the arrival of peace or, quite specifically, a change of fortune for the better. If the spark then pops and flies up, a letter or communication can be expected – something that announces a good offer or an opportunity that will broaden into a time of growing personal peace and tranquillity.

CORAL

Like fish, corals have an especially powerful and sacred connection with the sea and its gods. Here is a ritual you can do if your inner sense of calm has been disturbed, and especially if you are having bad dreams.

Choose a necklace of coral beads and place it for 24 hours in a bowl of rose petals. The next night, hang the coral beads around your neck or on the end of your bed, and strew the rose petals inside your pillow case. Surround yourself with coral-coloured light in your thoughts. This, together with the beads, will bring you peaceful dreams and a vision of how to proceed in the future.

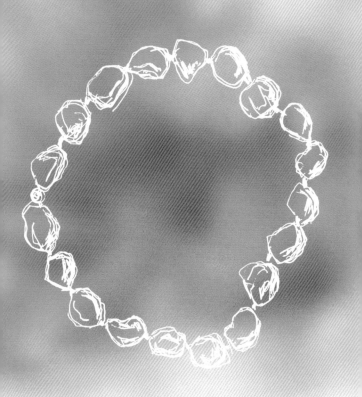

DIAMOND

These precious stones have a long history of use in witchcraft, as do many gemstones. This is a little ritual for peace and security, or even to end a quarrel with someone you love.

On the night of a storm, take a diamond, wrap it in a soft cloth, and rub it thrice. Place it underneath your pillow, and wish quietly as follows: "May peace now attend me in the night, and happiness enter at dawn of daylight." Not only will the morning bring better fortune and clear weather, but your dreams may give you very helpful advice during the night. The storm and the diamond together will clear up the strife.

Corn dolly

These are magical people indeed! The luckiest corn
dolls are made with the last little bit of corn from
the harvest; but any gift of a corn doll will be lucky
for you.

If you are given a present of a little corn doll, first thank the
bearer with a gift of silver, such as a little pin or small brooch.
Next, immediately give the doll a name of just one syllable –
Rose, Jane, Meg, and so on. Say quietly: "Bring golden sunshine
to our house", and place the doll in the rafters of the roof. Wish
very sweetly for peace and joy as you do it. The little doll should
be kept safe there always – a guardian of your hopes and dreams.

Dreams

Always ask a question outright if something is disturbing your peace.

In a still moment at bedtime, sit quietly and with a soft voice impart your troubles to Diana, the moon goddess. Ask that in your dreams she illuminate your understanding, and show you how to find a peaceful conclusion to whatever has been troubling you. You will dream a dream enveloped in a soft, moonlit glow. In the morning, you will have had some important message of how to find happiness – or where your happiness lies. Do not tell your dream to anyone at all until you have eaten your breakfast – for then, the dream is sure to come true.

EGG

This is probably only for country girls and boys –
unless you know someone who keeps hens. If you
have an important day ahead, ensure its success with
the following ritual.

Take the first egg of the day to be laid by a hen, carry it gently
to the house, cook it lovingly, then eat it for breakfast. This egg
is thought to be especially lucky, and will give you a day free
from frustration, argument or disappointment. For luck, keep
some of the pieces of shell and place them around the base of
a flowering plant.

A HORSEMAN

Possibly because of the connection with knights of old, a horseman was considered to be a lucky token if met on an important day. Some girls contrived to have a horse and rider meet them deliberately on their way to church on their wedding day. If you meet a horseman in the road, do this little spell for a week of complete peace.

Close your eyes when you see the horseman and quickly wish for peace and contentment. Tap your foot three times on the ground, and say: "Lucky horse, fleet of foot, May you be an omen good." Don't watch the horse disappear – seeing the tail end means you may only have the tail end of something good, rather than the whole.

According to custom, your week will turn out especially well.

Spark

This is a ritual for anyone with an open fireplace.

If you see a long spark of fire rise up the chimney quite suddenly, when the rest of the fire has been calm and burning evenly, you should soon have some good news concerning something that has been troubling you. Link little fingers with someone else, and wish hard for a happy resolution and the restoration of peaceful feelings.

The fire should now burn calmly again and, in the morning, you will hear something that pleases you.

Hydrangeas

Beautiful flowering hydrangeas in the garden
betoken love.

For a peaceful childhood for the younger members of a household,
it is unlucky to plant a hydrangea beside the front door (put a
myrtle there instead). Plant the hydrangea elsewhere in the
garden and your children will give you peace rather than bother.
If the flowers are blue, you will have more boys in the family,
and if pink, more girls (of course).

For peaceful weddings, it is lucky to take from one to three
blooms from a blue hydrangea and add this to a daughter's
bridal bouquet; the colour can be very pale. Tie the stems with
a blue ribbon and add other flowers from your own garden,
even if a florist is making up the bouquet.

Soap

The most desirable little commodity for weekends away and nice bathrooms at home. Follow this advice if you want to avoid any disruption to your peaceful holiday or away break. "Soap must not be left behind, Or you may have no peace of mind."

Take your own favourite soap with you, and a little piece of waxed or foil paper in which to wrap it and take it home again. This is equally true if you're staying in a hotel: always be sure to take away the soap. As you wrap it back into the little piece of paper, wish for a peaceful and trouble-free time until you return home, then when you're back home use up the bit of soap in a long peaceful bath or shower. Wrap any final remaining little piece in a few rose petals before you throw it away: this retains the peace and good luck.

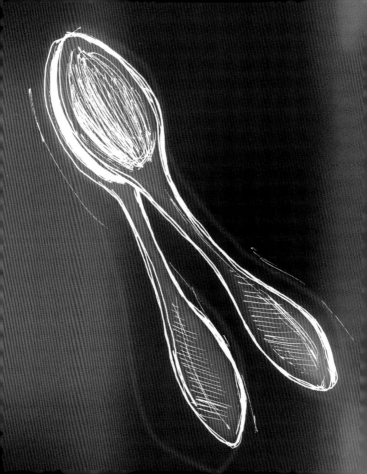

Two spoons

If two spoons somehow come to be placed together
on your saucer or in your cup, you must quickly
wish for the peaceful union of two lovers who have
been in discord. It may be that it affects you yourself
and your beloved the most. Place the spoons one
inside the other after your wish, and see what the
morrow brings.

TEA LEAF

Hard to find in a world hooked on the convenience of tea bags, this is one for those of us who still like to use real tea.

If you find that one lone tea leaf floats to the surface of your teacup, take it out at once on a spoon, then place it on the back of your hand. The leaf itself indicates that a stranger will come into your life who will bring something peaceful, possibly love, in the days ahead. Bump the palm of the free hand over the hand with the leaf on it. If the leaf sticks to the palm, the visitor will change your life and take away all your troubles.

SALT

Witches set a great deal of store by salt – and this seems to be a universal tradition. Try this for peace, as near as possible to May Day (May 1).

Place a tablespoon of salt into each of five cups, then add a few drops of food colouring to each one, making the first red/pink, the second orange/yellow, then green, then blue, then violet. Allow the salt to dry, then put each, one by one, in layers into a tightly corked jar. Tie with a white ribbon, then put the jar somewhere safe, where it can ever after bring peace, or the restoration of peace, to you and your home.

On the first day of each year, scatter some salt to the wind in your garden, or from a window. Wish peace to those all around you, and to you and yours.

Nine stars

After a very serious break-up with someone, you could try this wish ritual. It is considered very lucky for restoring peace, and will certainly reveal whether there's any future in the relationship.

Each night, for nine nights following your break-up, look out for the first nine stars to appear in the sky. On each one in turn, make a wish for kindness, truth, faith, affection, trust, strength, amity, forgiveness and better understanding. Do this for nine nights. On the tenth, you will discover whether your love has a bond strong enough to endure.

BEES

These little carriers of all kinds of omens seem to
have a close connection with the human mind. They
are renowned as harbingers of plenty and prosperity,
but also of a death in the family. It pays to treat them
respectfully if they enter your home.

When a bee flies in your window, on no account should you kill
it! Treat the visitor kindly and tell it of any concerns you have
regarding a quarrel with someone dear. Go and tie a brightly
coloured ribbon near the window through which the bee flew in,
and allow the bee to leave entirely of its own accord: do not chase
it out. If you notice its departure, say to it: "Mr Bee, Mr Bee, be
on your happy way, Bring me a happy end to this fine day."

Before the day is finished, your quarrel will start to mend.

MISTLETOE

We know we should kiss under a bough of mistletoe, but the druids thought this the most powerful of plants. Save a piece of mistletoe from Christmas and do the following.

Place a last sprig of the bough above the mantelpiece or front door, saying: "Oh mistletoe bough, daughter of the noblest of trees, ensure my prosperity and my peace in this year that is now dawning." The sprig should be kept until a new one is brought in at the following Yuletide, and then the old may be burnt. A steady flame presages a year ahead of steady peace and prosperity.

COIN

This bears a relationship with the earlier wish for luck concerning the coin and the fishing rod.

When you have had a bad quarrel with your beloved, take an especially shiny coin straight to the sea, or a river if you are too far from the ocean. Toss it backwards over your shoulder into the water, saying: "Never a backward glance at our anger, End our quarrel and end our danger." Imagine the shiny sparks of cross words dissolving in a sea of good feeling.

The quarrel should be over within three days if performed on a full moon, or a little longer if the moon was waxing.

Teapot

I love teapots, so this is a favourite ritual for a wish.

If you have had an argument with someone close and you want to make it up very fast, go to the teapot in which you usually make tea to drink together. Put your tea into the pot and make a wish for peace between you; pour on the boiling water, wait one minute exactly, then turn the teapot widdershins (anticlockwise) three times, asking that you unsay harsh words between you, and unmake the trouble. Wait one minute, then turn the teapot once more, one revolution only, in the sunwise (clockwise) direction, saying: "Come back to peace restored, and take a cup of tea with me."

Drink the tea and think warmly of your friend: the spell will work quickly to 'unlock' the trouble.

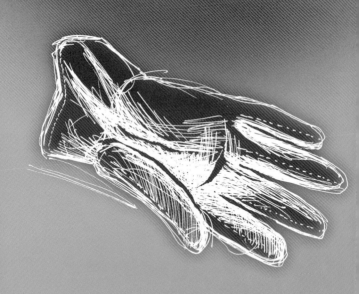

GLOVES

Some people feel that gloves are unlucky if they're dropped. This ritual probably derives from that idea.

If you drop a glove, ask another person to pick it up for you, and as they return it to your hand, clasp hands with them and make a wish. It is traditional to make a wish for a coming together of minds: perhaps you have not seen eye to eye with someone lately or, at times of national and international strife, you could make a wish for peace. The wish should be closed by a linking of little fingers.

First published in 2002 by
Quadrille Publishing Limited
Alhambra House
27-31 Charing Cross Road
London WC2H OLS

Reprinted in 2002

EDITOR Anne Furniss
DESIGN Jim Smith
PRODUCTION Tracy Hart, Vincent Smith

British Library Cataloguing in Publication Data
A catalogue record for this book is available
from the British Library

ISBN 1 903845 88 2

Printed in Hong Kong

10 9 8 7 6 5 4 3 2